Christmas Archive

THIS IS THE STORY OF:

D1519073

If found please return to:

_____

_____

_____

_____

Welcome!

Welcome to The Archive Hive - the place to write down all your holiday memories year after year! This Archive Hive product is more than just a journal - it's a keepsake to be passed down. It is designed to help you reflect on the happiness and struggles of years past as well as celebrate the present!

Our story

Growing up, our founder loved sitting at her grandparent's kitchen table and flipping through their collection of photo albums. The albums were full to bursting and sparked a love for keeping family history that inspires her work today. The Archive Hive's mission is to help you capture that feeling by archiving Your Story in a unique and special way.

How to Archive

The process is simple and the idea is this: 25 years of Christmas in one journal. Keep your journal tucked away with your Christmas decorations. Year after year you can flip through Your Story and joyfully recall past holidays. As each season closes, it takes just a few dedicated moments to add to your archive. The journal includes short writing prompts and provides an easy way to capture years of memories. The journal provides four pages per year for a total of twenty-five years of Christmas memories!

#TheArchiveHive family

At The Archive Hive, we love sharing memories and are fascinated by the way families celebrate and how each family holds different and special traditions near and dear. We celebrate these things in our online community by sharing images and stories from around the world. Join us to hear and share incredible stories!

THEARCHIVEHIVE.COM   @THEARCHIVEHIVE   /THEARCHIVEHIVE   /THEARCHIVEHIVE

YEAR:

DAY OF THE WEEK:

WEATHER:

NUMBER OF TREES DECORATED:

Christmas Archive

RECORD YOUR HOLIDAY MEMORIES

Talk about how you decorated for Christmas this year. New tree, old tree, outdoor decor? Do you have a decorating tradition? Did you add any new decorations this year?

Share your holiday meal and baking schedule this year. Did you decorate cookies or make a favorite dessert? Did you prepare specific items for a holiday meal? What other food items were notable this year?

What events and special parties led up to the holiday this year? Did you have any special celebrations or ceremonies to attend?

FIRST TO WAKE CHRISTMAS MORNING:

FAVORITE GIFT OF THE SEASON:

MISHAP MOMENT:

SPECIAL ORNAMENT THIS YEAR:

Christmas Archive

How did you spend Christmas Eve and Christmas Day? Which family and friends were in attendance?

_____

_____

_____

_____

_____

Talk about your outfits and attire this year. Did you do family jammies? Were there special dresses or suits worn to your celebrations?

_____

_____

_____

_____

Let's talk gifts. Were there any favorites this year or anything given or recieved that helped make this Christmas special?

_____

_____

_____

_____

_____

CHRISTMAS BOOK THIS YEAR:

CHRISTMAS SONG THIS YEAR:

CHRISTMAS MOVIE THIS YEAR:

TOP NEWS HEADLINE THIS YEAR:

Describe your new and old family traditions this year.

Use this space to describe your favorite holiday memory from this season.

Christmas Archive

PASTE YOUR HOLIDAY PHOTOS OR CARD HERE

YEAR:

DAY OF THE WEEK:

WEATHER:

NUMBER OF TREES DECORATED:

Christmas Archive

RECORD YOUR HOLIDAY MEMORIES

Talk about how you decorated for Christmas this year. New tree, old tree, outdoor decor? Do you have a decorating tradition? Did you add any new decorations this year?

Share your holiday meal and baking schedule this year. Did you decorate cookies or make a favorite dessert? Did you prepare specific items for a holiday meal? What other food items were notable this year?

What events and special parties led up to the holiday this year? Did you have any special celebrations or ceremonies to attend?

FIRST TO WAKE CHRISTMAS MORNING:

FAVORITE GIFT OF THE SEASON:

MISHAP MOMENT

SPECIAL ORNAMENT THIS YEAR:

Christmas Archive

How did you spend Christmas Eve and Christmas Day? Which family and friends were in attendance?

_____

_____

_____

_____

_____

Talk about your outfits and attire this year. Did you do family jammies? Were there special dresses or suits worn to your celebrations?

_____

_____

_____

_____

_____

Let's talk gifts. Were there any favorites this year or anything given or recieved that helped make this Christmas special?

_____

_____

_____

_____

_____

CHRISTMAS BOOK THIS YEAR:

CHRISTMAS SONG THIS YEAR:

CHRISTMAS MOVIE THIS YEAR:

TOP NEWS HEADLINE THIS YEAR:

Describe your new and old family traditions this year.

Use this space to describe your favorite holiday memory from this season.

Christmas Archive

PASTE YOUR HOLIDAY PHOTOS OR CARD HERE

YEAR:

DAY OF THE WEEK:

WEATHER:

NUMBER OF TREES DECORATED:

Christmas Archive

RECORD YOUR HOLIDAY MEMORIES

Talk about how you decorated for Christmas this year. New tree, old tree, outdoor decor? Do you have a decorating tradition? Did you add any new decorations this year?

Share your holiday meal and baking schedule this year. Did you decorate cookies or make a favorite dessert? Did you prepare specific items for a holiday meal? What other food items were notable this year?

What events and special parties led up to the holiday this year? Did you have any special celebrations or ceremonies to attend?

FIRST TO WAKE CHRISTMAS MORNING:

FAVORITE GIFT OF THE SEASON:

MISHAP MOMENT:

SPECIAL ORNAMENT THIS YEAR:

Christmas Archive

How did you spend Christmas Eve and Christmas Day? Which family and friends were in attendance?

_____

_____

_____

_____

_____

Talk about your outfits and attire this year. Did you do family jammies? Were there special dresses or suits worn to your celebrations?

_____

_____

_____

_____

Let's talk gifts. Were there any favorites this year or anything given or recieved that helped make this Christmas special?

_____

_____

_____

_____

_____

CHRISTMAS BOOK THIS YEAR:

CHRISTMAS SONG THIS YEAR:

CHRISTMAS MOVIE THIS YEAR:

TOP NEWS HEADLINE THIS YEAR:

Describe your new and old family traditions this year.

Use this space to describe your favorite holiday memory from this season.

Christmas Archive

PASTE YOUR HOLIDAY PHOTOS OR CARD HERE

YEAR:

DAY OF THE WEEK:

WEATHER:

NUMBER OF TREES DECORATED:

Christmas Archive

RECORD YOUR HOLIDAY MEMORIES

Talk about how you decorated for Christmas this year. New tree, old tree, outdoor decor? Do you have a decorating tradition? Did you add any new decorations this year?

Share your holiday meal and baking schedule this year. Did you decorate cookies or make a favorite dessert? Did you prepare specific items for a holiday meal? What other food items were notable this year?

What events and special parties led up to the holiday this year? Did you have any special celebrations or ceremonies to attend?

FIRST TO WAKE CHRISTMAS MORNING:

FAVORITE GIFT OF THE SEASON:

MISHAP MOMENT:

SPECIAL ORNAMENT THIS YEAR:

Christmas Archive

How did you spend Christmas Eve and Christmas Day? Which family and friends were in attendance?

_____

_____

_____

_____

_____

Talk about your outfits and attire this year. Did you do family jammies? Were there special dresses or suits worn to your celebrations?

_____

_____

_____

_____

_____

Let's talk gifts. Were there any favorites this year or anything given or recieved that helped make this Christmas special?

_____

_____

_____

_____

_____

CHRISTMAS BOOK THIS YEAR:

CHRISTMAS SONG THIS YEAR:

CHRISTMAS MOVIE THIS YEAR:

TOP NEWS HEADLINE THIS YEAR:

Describe your new and old family traditions this year.

Use this space to describe your favorite holiday memory from this season.

Christmas Archive

PASTE YOUR HOLIDAY PHOTOS OR CARD HERE

YEAR:

DAY OF THE WEEK:

WEATHER:

NUMBER OF TREES DECORATED:

Christmas Archive

RECORD YOUR HOLIDAY MEMORIES

Talk about how you decorated for Christmas this year. New tree, old tree, outdoor decor? Do you have a decorating tradition? Did you add any new decorations this year?

_____

_____

_____

_____

_____

_____

Share your holiday meal and baking schedule this year. Did you decorate cookies or make a favorite dessert? Did you prepare specific items for a holiday meal? What other food items were notable this year?

_____

_____

_____

_____

_____

What events and special parties led up to the holiday this year? Did you have any special celebrations or ceremonies to attend?

_____

_____

_____

_____

FIRST TO WAKE CHRISTMAS MORNING:

FAVORITE GIFT OF THE SEASON:

MISHAP MOMENT:

SPECIAL ORNAMENT THIS YEAR:

Christmas Archive

How did you spend Christmas Eve and Christmas Day? Which family and friends were in attendance?

_____

_____

_____

_____

_____

Talk about your outfits and attire this year. Did you do family jammies? Were there special dresses or suits worn to your celebrations?

_____

_____

_____

_____

_____

Let's talk gifts. Were there any favorites this year or anything given or recieved that helped make this Christmas special?

_____

_____

_____

_____

_____

CHRISTMAS BOOK THIS YEAR:

CHRISTMAS SONG THIS YEAR:

CHRISTMAS MOVIE THIS YEAR:

TOP NEWS HEADLINE THIS YEAR:

Describe your new and old family traditions this year.

Use this space to describe your favorite holiday memory from this season.

Christmas Archive

PASTE YOUR HOLIDAY PHOTOS OR CARD HERE

YEAR:

DAY OF THE WEEK:

WEATHER:

NUMBER OF TREES DECORATED:

Christmas Archive

RECORD YOUR HOLIDAY MEMORIES

Talk about how you decorated for Christmas this year. New tree, old tree, outdoor decor? Do you have a decorating tradition? Did you add any new decorations this year?

_____

_____

_____

_____

Share your holiday meal and baking schedule this year. Did you decorate cookies or make a favorite dessert? Did you prepare specific items for a holiday meal? What other food items were notable this year?

_____

_____

_____

_____

What events and special parties led up to the holiday this year? Did you have any special celebrations or ceremonies to attend?

_____

_____

_____

FIRST TO WAKE CHRISTMAS MORNING:

FAVORITE GIFT OF THE SEASON:

MISHAP MOMENT:

SPECIAL ORNAMENT THIS YEAR:

Christmas Archive

How did you spend Christmas Eve and Christmas Day? Which family and friends were in attendance?

_____

_____

_____

_____

Talk about your outfits and attire this year. Did you do family jammies? Were there special dresses or suits worn to your celebrations?

_____

_____

_____

_____

Let's talk gifts. Were there any favorites this year or anything given or recieved that helped make this Christmas special?

_____

_____

_____

_____

CHRISTMAS BOOK THIS YEAR:

CHRISTMAS SONG THIS YEAR:

CHRISTMAS MOVIE THIS YEAR:

TOP NEWS HEADLINE THIS YEAR:

Describe your new and old family traditions this year.

Use this space to describe your favorite holiday memory from this season.

Christmas Archive

PASTE YOUR HOLIDAY PHOTOS OR CARD HERE

YEAR:

DAY OF THE WEEK:

WEATHER:

NUMBER OF TREES DECORATED:

Christmas Archive

RECORD YOUR HOLIDAY MEMORIES

Talk about how you decorated for Christmas this year. New tree, old tree, outdoor decor? Do you have a decorating tradition? Did you add any new decorations this year?

_____

_____

_____

_____

_____

Share your holiday meal and baking schedule this year. Did you decorate cookies or make a favorite dessert? Did you prepare specific items for a holiday meal? What other food items were notable this year?

_____

_____

_____

_____

_____

What events and special parties led up to the holiday this year? Did you have any special celebrations or ceremonies to attend?

_____

_____

_____

_____

FIRST TO WAKE CHRISTMAS MORNING:

FAVORITE GIFT OF THE SEASON:

MISHAP MOMENT:

SPECIAL ORNAMENT THIS YEAR:

Christmas Archive

How did you spend Christmas Eve and Christmas Day? Which family and friends were in attendance?

Talk about your outfits and attire this year. Did you do family jammies? Were there special dresses or suits worn to your celebrations?

Let's talk gifts. Were there any favorites this year or anything given or recieved that helped make this Christmas special?

CHRISTMAS BOOK THIS YEAR:

CHRISTMAS SONG THIS YEAR:

CHRISTMAS MOVIE THIS YEAR:

TOP NEWS HEADLINE THIS YEAR:

Describe your new and old family traditions this year.

Use this space to describe your favorite holiday memory from this season.

Christmas Archive

YEAR:

DAY OF THE WEEK:

WEATHER:

NUMBER OF TREES DECORATED:

Christmas Archive

RECORD YOUR HOLIDAY MEMORIES

Talk about how you decorated for Christmas this year. New tree, old tree, outdoor decor? Do you have a decorating tradition? Did you add any new decorations this year?

Share your holiday meal and baking schedule this year. Did you decorate cookies or make a favorite dessert? Did you prepare specific items for a holiday meal? What other food items were notable this year?

What events and special parties led up to the holiday this year? Did you have any special celebrations or ceremonies to attend?

FIRST TO WAKE CHRISTMAS MORNING:

FAVORITE GIFT OF THE SEASON:

MISHAP MOMENT:

SPECIAL ORNAMENT THIS YEAR:

Christmas Archive

How did you spend Christmas Eve and Christmas Day? Which family and friends were in attendance?

_____

_____

_____

_____

_____

Talk about your outfits and attire this year. Did you do family jammies? Were there special dresses or suits worn to your celebrations?

_____

_____

_____

_____

Let's talk gifts. Were there any favorites this year or anything given or recieved that helped make this Christmas special?

_____

_____

_____

_____

_____

CHRISTMAS BOOK THIS YEAR:

CHRISTMAS SONG THIS YEAR:

CHRISTMAS MOVIE THIS YEAR:

TOP NEWS HEADLINE THIS YEAR:

Describe your new and old family traditions this year.

Use this space to describe your favorite holiday memory from this season.

Christmas Archive

PASTE YOUR HOLIDAY PHOTOS OR CARD HERE

YEAR:

DAY OF THE WEEK:

WEATHER:

NUMBER OF TREES DECORATED:

Christmas Archive

RECORD YOUR HOLIDAY MEMORIES

Talk about how you decorated for Christmas this year. New tree, old tree, outdoor decor? Do you have a decorating tradition? Did you add any new decorations this year?

_____

_____

_____

_____

_____

_____

Share your holiday meal and baking schedule this year. Did you decorate cookies or make a favorite dessert? Did you prepare specific items for a holiday meal? What other food items were notable this year?

_____

_____

_____

_____

_____

_____

What events and special parties led up to the holiday this year? Did you have any special celebrations or ceremonies to attend?

_____

_____

_____

_____

FIRST TO WAKE CHRISTMAS MORNING:

FAVORITE GIFT OF THE SEASON:

MISHAP MOMENT:

SPECIAL ORNAMENT THIS YEAR:

Christmas Archive

How did you spend Christmas Eve and Christmas Day? Which family and friends were in attendance?

_____

_____

_____

_____

_____

Talk about your outfits and attire this year. Did you do family jammies? Were there special dresses or suits worn to your celebrations?

_____

_____

_____

_____

Let's talk gifts. Were there any favorites this year or anything given or recieved that helped make this Christmas special?

_____

_____

_____

_____

_____

CHRISTMAS BOOK THIS YEAR:

CHRISTMAS SONG THIS YEAR:

CHRISTMAS MOVIE THIS YEAR:

TOP NEWS HEADLINE THIS YEAR:

Describe your new and old family traditions this year.

Use this space to describe your favorite holiday memory from this season.

Christmas Archive

PASTE YOUR HOLIDAY PHOTOS OR CARD HERE

YEAR:

DAY OF THE WEEK:

WEATHER:

NUMBER OF TREES DECORATED:

Christmas Archive

RECORD YOUR HOLIDAY MEMORIES

Talk about how you decorated for Christmas this year. New tree, old tree, outdoor decor? Do you have a decorating tradition? Did you add any new decorations this year?

Share your holiday meal and baking schedule this year. Did you decorate cookies or make a favorite dessert? Did you prepare specific items for a holiday meal? What other food items were notable this year?

What events and special parties led up to the holiday this year? Did you have any special celebrations or ceremonies to attend?

FIRST TO WAKE CHRISTMAS MORNING:

FAVORITE GIFT OF THE SEASON:

MISHAP MOMENT:

SPECIAL ORNAMENT THIS YEAR:

Christmas Archive

How did you spend Christmas Eve and Christmas Day? Which family and friends were in attendance?

_____

_____

_____

_____

_____

Talk about your outfits and attire this year. Did you do family jammies? Were there special dresses or suits worn to your celebrations?

_____

_____

_____

_____

Let's talk gifts. Were there any favorites this year or anything given or recieved that helped make this Christmas special?

_____

_____

_____

_____

_____

CHRISTMAS BOOK THIS YEAR:

CHRISTMAS SONG THIS YEAR:

CHRISTMAS MOVIE THIS YEAR:

TOP NEWS HEADLINE THIS YEAR:

Describe your new and old family traditions this year.

Use this space to describe your favorite holiday memory from this season.

Christmas Archive

YEAR:

DAY OF THE WEEK:

WEATHER:

NUMBER OF TREES DECORATED:

Christmas Archive

RECORD YOUR HOLIDAY MEMORIES

Talk about how you decorated for Christmas this year. New tree, old tree, outdoor decor? Do you have a decorating tradition? Did you add any new decorations this year?

_____

_____

_____

_____

_____

Share your holiday meal and baking schedule this year. Did you decorate cookies or make a favorite dessert? Did you prepare specific items for a holiday meal? What other food items were notable this year?

_____

_____

_____

_____

_____

What events and special parties led up to the holiday this year? Did you have any special celebrations or ceremonies to attend?

_____

_____

_____

_____

FIRST TO WAKE CHRISTMAS MORNING:

FAVORITE GIFT OF THE SEASON:

MISHAP MOMENT:

SPECIAL ORNAMENT THIS YEAR:

Christmas Archive

How did you spend Christmas Eve and Christmas Day? Which family and friends were in attendance?

_____

_____

_____

_____

_____

Talk about your outfits and attire this year. Did you do family jammies? Were there special dresses or suits worn to your celebrations?

_____

_____

_____

_____

Let's talk gifts. Were there any favorites this year or anything given or recieved that helped make this Christmas special?

_____

_____

_____

_____

CHRISTMAS BOOK THIS YEAR:

CHRISTMAS SONG THIS YEAR:

CHRISTMAS MOVIE THIS YEAR:

TOP NEWS HEADLINE THIS YEAR:

Describe your new and old family traditions this year.

Use this space to describe your favorite holiday memory from this season.

Christmas Archive

PASTE YOUR HOLIDAY PHOTOS OR CARD HERE

YEAR:

DAY OF THE WEEK:

WEATHER:

NUMBER OF TREES DECORATED:

Christmas Archive

RECORD YOUR HOLIDAY MEMORIES

Talk about how you decorated for Christmas this year. New tree, old tree, outdoor decor? Do you have a decorating tradition? Did you add any new decorations this year?

_____

_____

_____

_____

_____

Share your holiday meal and baking schedule this year. Did you decorate cookies or make a favorite dessert? Did you prepare specific items for a holiday meal? What other food items were notable this year?

_____

_____

_____

_____

_____

What events and special parties led up to the holiday this year? Did you have any special celebrations or ceremonies to attend?

_____

_____

_____

_____

FIRST TO WAKE CHRISTMAS MORNING:

FAVORITE GIFT OF THE SEASON:

MISHAP MOMENT:

SPECIAL ORNAMENT THIS YEAR:

Christmas Archive

How did you spend Christmas Eve and Christmas Day? Which family and friends were in attendance?

_____

_____

_____

_____

_____

Talk about your outfits and attire this year. Did you do family jammies? Were there special dresses or suits worn to your celebrations?

_____

_____

_____

_____

Let's talk gifts. Were there any favorites this year or anything given or recieved that helped make this Christmas special?

_____

_____

_____

_____

_____

CHRISTMAS BOOK THIS YEAR:

CHRISTMAS SONG THIS YEAR:

CHRISTMAS MOVIE THIS YEAR:

TOP NEWS HEADLINE THIS YEAR:

Describe your new and old family traditions this year.

Use this space to describe your favorite holiday memory from this season.

Christmas Archive

PASTE YOUR HOLIDAY PHOTOS OR CARD HERE

YEAR:

DAY OF THE WEEK:

WEATHER:

NUMBER OF TREES DECORATED:

Christmas Archive

RECORD YOUR HOLIDAY MEMORIES

Talk about how you decorated for Christmas this year. New tree, old tree, outdoor decor? Do you have a decorating tradition? Did you add any new decorations this year?

_____

_____

_____

_____

_____

_____

Share your holiday meal and baking schedule this year. Did you decorate cookies or make a favorite dessert? Did you prepare specific items for a holiday meal? What other food items were notable this year?

_____

_____

_____

_____

_____

_____

What events and special parties led up to the holiday this year? Did you have any special celebrations or ceremonies to attend?

_____

_____

_____

_____

FIRST TO WAKE CHRISTMAS MORNING:

FAVORITE GIFT OF THE SEASON:

MISHAP MOMENT:

SPECIAL ORNAMENT THIS YEAR:

Christmas Archive

How did you spend Christmas Eve and Christmas Day? Which family and friends were in attendance?

_____

_____

_____

_____

_____

Talk about your outfits and attire this year. Did you do family jammies? Were there special dresses or suits worn to your celebrations?

_____

_____

_____

_____

Let's talk gifts. Were there any favorites this year or anything given or recieved that helped make this Christmas special?

_____

_____

_____

_____

_____

CHRISTMAS BOOK THIS YEAR:

CHRISTMAS SONG THIS YEAR:

CHRISTMAS MOVIE THIS YEAR:

TOP NEWS HEADLINE THIS YEAR:

Describe your new and old family traditions this year.

Use this space to describe your favorite holiday memory from this season.

Christmas Archive

PASTE YOUR HOLIDAY PHOTOS OR CARD HERE

YEAR:

DAY OF THE WEEK:

WEATHER:

NUMBER OF TREES DECORATED:

Christmas Archive

RECORD YOUR HOLIDAY MEMORIES

Talk about how you decorated for Christmas this year. New tree, old tree, outdoor decor? Do you have a decorating tradition? Did you add any new decorations this year?

Share your holiday meal and baking schedule this year. Did you decorate cookies or make a favorite dessert? Did you prepare specific items for a holiday meal? What other food items were notable this year?

What events and special parties led up to the holiday this year? Did you have any special celebrations or ceremonies to attend?

FIRST TO WAKE CHRISTMAS MORNING:

FAVORITE GIFT OF THE SEASON:

MISHAP MOMENT:

SPECIAL ORNAMENT THIS YEAR:

Christmas Archive

How did you spend Christmas Eve and Christmas Day? Which family and friends were in attendance?

_____

_____

_____

_____

_____

Talk about your outfits and attire this year. Did you do family jammies? Were there special dresses or suits worn to your celebrations?

_____

_____

_____

_____

Let's talk gifts. Were there any favorites this year or anything given or recieved that helped make this Christmas special?

_____

_____

_____

_____

_____

CHRISTMAS BOOK THIS YEAR:

CHRISTMAS SONG THIS YEAR:

CHRISTMAS MOVIE THIS YEAR:

TOP NEWS HEADLINE THIS YEAR:

Describe your new and old family traditions this year.

Use this space to describe your favorite holiday memory from this season.

Christmas Archive

YEAR:

DAY OF THE WEEK:

WEATHER:

NUMBER OF TREES DECORATED:

Christmas Archive

RECORD YOUR HOLIDAY MEMORIES

Talk about how you decorated for Christmas this year. New tree, old tree, outdoor decor? Do you have a decorating tradition? Did you add any new decorations this year?

Share your holiday meal and baking schedule this year. Did you decorate cookies or make a favorite dessert? Did you prepare specific items for a holiday meal? What other food items were notable this year?

What events and special parties led up to the holiday this year? Did you have any special celebrations or ceremonies to attend?

FIRST TO WAKE CHRISTMAS MORNING:

FAVORITE GIFT OF THE SEASON:

MISHAP MOMENT:

SPECIAL ORNAMENT THIS YEAR:

Christmas Archive

How did you spend Christmas Eve and Christmas Day? Which family and friends were in attendance?

_____

_____

_____

_____

_____

_____

Talk about your outfits and attire this year. Did you do family jammies? Were there special dresses or suits worn to your celebrations?

_____

_____

_____

_____

_____

_____

Let's talk gifts. Were there any favorites this year or anything given or recieved that helped make this Christmas special?

_____

_____

_____

_____

_____

_____

CHRISTMAS BOOK THIS YEAR:

CHRISTMAS SONG THIS YEAR:

CHRISTMAS MOVIE THIS YEAR:

TOP NEWS HEADLINE THIS YEAR:

Describe your new and old family traditions this year.

Use this space to describe your favorite holiday memory from this season.

Christmas Archive

YEAR:

DAY OF THE WEEK:

WEATHER:

NUMBER OF TREES DECORATED:

Christmas Archive

RECORD YOUR HOLIDAY MEMORIES

Talk about how you decorated for Christmas this year. New tree, old tree, outdoor decor? Do you have a decorating tradition? Did you add any new decorations this year?

Share your holiday meal and baking schedule this year. Did you decorate cookies or make a favorite dessert? Did you prepare specific items for a holiday meal? What other food items were notable this year?

What events and special parties led up to the holiday this year? Did you have any special celebrations or ceremonies to attend?

FIRST TO WAKE CHRISTMAS MORNING:

FAVORITE GIFT OF THE SEASON:

MISHAP MOMENT:

SPECIAL ORNAMENT THIS YEAR:

Christmas Archive

How did you spend Christmas Eve and Christmas Day? Which family and friends were in attendance?

Talk about your outfits and attire this year. Did you do family jammies? Were there special dresses or suits worn to your celebrations?

Let's talk gifts. Were there any favorites this year or anything given or recieved that helped make this Christmas special?

CHRISTMAS BOOK THIS YEAR:

CHRISTMAS SONG THIS YEAR:

CHRISTMAS MOVIE THIS YEAR:

TOP NEWS HEADLINE THIS YEAR:

Describe your new and old family traditions this year.

Use this space to describe your favorite holiday memory from this season.

Christmas Archive

PASTE YOUR HOLIDAY PHOTOS OR CARD HERE

YEAR:

DAY OF THE WEEK:

WEATHER:

NUMBER OF TREES DECORATED:

Christmas Archive

RECORD YOUR HOLIDAY MEMORIES

Talk about how you decorated for Christmas this year. New tree, old tree, outdoor decor? Do you have a decorating tradition? Did you add any new decorations this year?

Share your holiday meal and baking schedule this year. Did you decorate cookies or make a favorite dessert? Did you prepare specific items for a holiday meal? What other food items were notable this year?

What events and special parties led up to the holiday this year? Did you have any special celebrations or ceremonies to attend?

FIRST TO WAKE CHRISTMAS MORNING:

FAVORITE GIFT OF THE SEASON:

MISHAP MOMENT:

SPECIAL ORNAMENT THIS YEAR:

Christmas Archive

How did you spend Christmas Eve and Christmas Day? Which family and friends were in attendance?

_____

_____

_____

_____

_____

_____

Talk about your outfits and attire this year. Did you do family jammies? Were there special dresses or suits worn to your celebrations?

_____

_____

_____

_____

_____

_____

Let's talk gifts. Were there any favorites this year or anything given or recieved that helped make this Christmas special?

_____

_____

_____

_____

_____

_____

CHRISTMAS BOOK THIS YEAR:

CHRISTMAS SONG THIS YEAR:

CHRISTMAS MOVIE THIS YEAR:

TOP NEWS HEADLINE THIS YEAR:

Describe your new and old family traditions this year.

Use this space to describe your favorite holiday memory from this season.

Christmas Archive

YEAR:

DAY OF THE WEEK:

WEATHER:

NUMBER OF TREES DECORATED:

Christmas Archive

RECORD YOUR HOLIDAY MEMORIES

Talk about how you decorated for Christmas this year. New tree, old tree, outdoor decor? Do you have a decorating tradition? Did you add any new decorations this year?

Share your holiday meal and baking schedule this year. Did you decorate cookies or make a favorite dessert? Did you prepare specific items for a holiday meal? What other food items were notable this year?

What events and special parties led up to the holiday this year? Did you have any special celebrations or ceremonies to attend?

FIRST TO WAKE CHRISTMAS MORNING:

FAVORITE GIFT OF THE SEASON:

MISHAP MOMENT:

SPECIAL ORNAMENT THIS YEAR:

Christmas Archive

How did you spend Christmas Eve and Christmas Day? Which family and friends were in attendance?

_____

_____

_____

_____

_____

_____

Talk about your outfits and attire this year. Did you do family jammies? Were there special dresses or suits worn to your celebrations?

_____

_____

_____

_____

_____

Let's talk gifts. Were there any favorites this year or anything given or recieved that helped make this Christmas special?

_____

_____

_____

_____

_____

CHRISTMAS BOOK THIS YEAR:

CHRISTMAS SONG THIS YEAR:

CHRISTMAS MOVIE THIS YEAR:

TOP NEWS HEADLINE THIS YEAR:

Describe your new and old family traditions this year.

Use this space to describe your favorite holiday memory from this season.

Christmas Archive

PASTE YOUR HOLIDAY PHOTOS OR CARD HERE

YEAR:

DAY OF THE WEEK:

WEATHER:

NUMBER OF TREES DECORATED:

Christmas Archive

RECORD YOUR HOLIDAY MEMORIES

Talk about how you decorated for Christmas this year. New tree, old tree, outdoor decor? Do you have a decorating tradition? Did you add any new decorations this year?

_____

_____

_____

_____

Share your holiday meal and baking schedule this year. Did you decorate cookies or make a favorite dessert? Did you prepare specific items for a holiday meal? What other food items were notable this year?

_____

_____

_____

_____

What events and special parties led up to the holiday this year? Did you have any special celebrations or ceremonies to attend?

_____

_____

_____

FIRST TO WAKE CHRISTMAS MORNING:

FAVORITE GIFT OF THE SEASON:

MISHAP MOMENT:

SPECIAL ORNAMENT THIS YEAR:

Christmas Archive

How did you spend Christmas Eve and Christmas Day? Which family and friends were in attendance?

_____

_____

_____

_____

_____

Talk about your outfits and attire this year. Did you do family jammies? Were there special dresses or suits worn to your celebrations?

_____

_____

_____

_____

Let's talk gifts. Were there any favorites this year or anything given or recieved that helped make this Christmas special?

_____

_____

_____

_____

_____

CHRISTMAS BOOK THIS YEAR:

CHRISTMAS SONG THIS YEAR:

CHRISTMAS MOVIE THIS YEAR:

TOP NEWS HEADLINE THIS YEAR:

Describe your new and old family traditions this year.

Use this space to describe your favorite holiday memory from this season.

Christmas Archive

YEAR:

DAY OF THE WEEK:

WEATHER:

NUMBER OF TREES DECORATED:

Christmas Archive

RECORD YOUR HOLIDAY MEMORIES

Talk about how you decorated for Christmas this year. New tree, old tree, outdoor decor? Do you have a decorating tradition? Did you add any new decorations this year?

_____

_____

_____

_____

_____

_____

Share your holiday meal and baking schedule this year. Did you decorate cookies or make a favorite dessert? Did you prepare specific items for a holiday meal? What other food items were notable this year?

_____

_____

_____

_____

_____

What events and special parties led up to the holiday this year? Did you have any special celebrations or ceremonies to attend?

_____

_____

_____

FIRST TO WAKE CHRISTMAS MORNING:

FAVORITE GIFT OF THE SEASON:

MISHAP MOMENT:

SPECIAL ORNAMENT THIS YEAR:

Christmas Archive

How did you spend Christmas Eve and Christmas Day? Which family and friends were in attendance?

_____

_____

_____

_____

_____

Talk about your outfits and attire this year. Did you do family jammies? Were there special dresses or suits worn to your celebrations?

_____

_____

_____

_____

_____

Let's talk gifts. Were there any favorites this year or anything given or recieved that helped make this Christmas special?

_____

_____

_____

_____

_____

CHRISTMAS BOOK THIS YEAR:

CHRISTMAS SONG THIS YEAR:

CHRISTMAS MOVIE THIS YEAR:

TOP NEWS HEADLINE THIS YEAR:

Describe your new and old family traditions this year.

Use this space to describe your favorite holiday memory from this season.

Christmas Archive

PASTE YOUR HOLIDAY PHOTOS OR CARD HERE

YEAR:

DAY OF THE WEEK:

WEATHER:

NUMBER OF TREES DECORATED:

Christmas Archive

RECORD YOUR HOLIDAY MEMORIES

Talk about how you decorated for Christmas this year. New tree, old tree, outdoor decor? Do you have a decorating tradition? Did you add any new decorations this year?

Share your holiday meal and baking schedule this year. Did you decorate cookies or make a favorite dessert? Did you prepare specific items for a holiday meal? What other food items were notable this year?

What events and special parties led up to the holiday this year? Did you have any special celebrations or ceremonies to attend?

FIRST TO WAKE CHRISTMAS MORNING:

FAVORITE GIFT OF THE SEASON:

MISHAP MOMENT:

SPECIAL ORNAMENT THIS YEAR:

Christmas Archive

How did you spend Christmas Eve and Christmas Day? Which family and friends were in attendance?

_____

_____

_____

_____

_____

Talk about your outfits and attire this year. Did you do family jammies? Were there special dresses or suits worn to your celebrations?

_____

_____

_____

_____

Let's talk gifts. Were there any favorites this year or anything given or recieved that helped make this Christmas special?

_____

_____

_____

_____

_____

CHRISTMAS BOOK THIS YEAR:

CHRISTMAS SONG THIS YEAR:

CHRISTMAS MOVIE THIS YEAR:

TOP NEWS HEADLINE THIS YEAR:

Describe your new and old family traditions this year.

Use this space to describe your favorite holiday memory from this season.

Christmas Archive

PASTE YOUR HOLIDAY PHOTOS OR CARD HERE

YEAR:

DAY OF THE WEEK:

WEATHER:

NUMBER OF TREES DECORATED:

Christmas Archive

RECORD YOUR HOLIDAY MEMORIES

Talk about how you decorated for Christmas this year. New tree, old tree, outdoor decor? Do you have a decorating tradition? Did you add any new decorations this year?

_____

_____

_____

_____

_____

Share your holiday meal and baking schedule this year. Did you decorate cookies or make a favorite dessert? Did you prepare specific items for a holiday meal? What other food items were notable this year?

_____

_____

_____

_____

_____

What events and special parties led up to the holiday this year? Did you have any special celebrations or ceremonies to attend?

_____

_____

_____

_____

FIRST TO WAKE CHRISTMAS MORNING:

FAVORITE GIFT OF THE SEASON:

MISHAP MOMENT:

SPECIAL ORNAMENT THIS YEAR:

Christmas Archive

How did you spend Christmas Eve and Christmas Day? Which family and friends were in attendance?

Talk about your outfits and attire this year. Did you do family jammies? Were there special dresses or suits worn to your celebrations?

Let's talk gifts. Were there any favorites this year or anything given or recieved that helped make this Christmas special?

CHRISTMAS BOOK THIS YEAR:

CHRISTMAS SONG THIS YEAR:

CHRISTMAS MOVIE THIS YEAR:

TOP NEWS HEADLINE THIS YEAR:

Describe your new and old family traditions this year.

Use this space to describe your favorite holiday memory from this season.

Christmas Archive

PASTE YOUR HOLIDAY PHOTOS OR CARD HERE

YEAR:

DAY OF THE WEEK:

WEATHER:

NUMBER OF TREES DECORATED:

Christmas Archive

RECORD YOUR HOLIDAY MEMORIES

Talk about how you decorated for Christmas this year. New tree, old tree, outdoor decor? Do you have a decorating tradition? Did you add any new decorations this year?

_____

_____

_____

_____

_____

Share your holiday meal and baking schedule this year. Did you decorate cookies or make a favorite dessert? Did you prepare specific items for a holiday meal? What other food items were notable this year?

_____

_____

_____

_____

What events and special parties led up to the holiday this year? Did you have any special celebrations or ceremonies to attend?

_____

_____

_____

_____

FIRST TO WAKE CHRISTMAS MORNING:

FAVORITE GIFT OF THE SEASON:

MISHAP MOMENT:

SPECIAL ORNAMENT THIS YEAR:

Christmas Archive

How did you spend Christmas Eve and Christmas Day? Which family and friends were in attendance?

_____

_____

_____

_____

_____

_____

Talk about your outfits and attire this year. Did you do family jammies? Were there special dresses or suits worn to your celebrations?

_____

_____

_____

_____

_____

_____

Let's talk gifts. Were there any favorites this year or anything given or recieved that helped make this Christmas special?

_____

_____

_____

_____

_____

_____

CHRISTMAS BOOK THIS YEAR:

CHRISTMAS SONG THIS YEAR:

CHRISTMAS MOVIE THIS YEAR:

TOP NEWS HEADLINE THIS YEAR:

Describe your new and old family traditions this year.

Use this space to describe your favorite holiday memory from this season.

Christmas Archive

PASTE YOUR HOLIDAY PHOTOS OR CARD HERE

EAR:

DAY OF THE WEEK:

VEATHER:

NUMBER OF TREES DECORATED:

Christmas Archive

RECORD YOUR HOLIDAY MEMORIES

alk about how you decorated for Christmas this year. New tree, old tree, outdoor decor? Do
ou have a decorating tradition? Did you add any new decorations this year?

hare your holiday meal and baking schedule this year. Did you decorate cookies or make a
avorite dessert? Did you prepare specific items for a holiday meal? What other food items
vere notable this year?

Vhat events and special parties led up to the holiday this year? Did you have any special
elebrations or ceremonies to attend?

FIRST TO WAKE CHRISTMAS MORNING:

FAVORITE GIFT OF THE SEASON:

MISHAP MOMENT:

SPECIAL ORNAMENT THIS YEAR:

Christmas Archive

How did you spend Christmas Eve and Christmas Day? Which family and friends were in attendance?

_____

_____

_____

_____

_____

Talk about your outfits and attire this year. Did you do family jammies? Were there special dresses or suits worn to your celebrations?

_____

_____

_____

_____

Let's talk gifts. Were there any favorites this year or anything given or recieved that helped make this Christmas special?

_____

_____

_____

_____

_____

CHRISTMAS BOOK THIS YEAR:

CHRISTMAS SONG THIS YEAR:

CHRISTMAS MOVIE THIS YEAR:

TOP NEWS HEADLINE THIS YEAR:

Describe your new and old family traditions this year.

Use this space to describe your favorite holiday memory from this season.

Christmas Archive

PASTE YOUR HOLIDAY PHOTOS OR CARD HERE

EAR:

DAY OF THE WEEK:

VEATHER:

NUMBER OF TREES DECORATED:

Christmas Archive

RECORD YOUR HOLIDAY MEMORIES

alk about how you decorated for Christmas this year. New tree, old tree, outdoor decor? Do
ou have a decorating tradition? Did you add any new decorations this year?

_____

_____

_____

_____

_____

_____

hare your holiday meal and baking schedule this year. Did you decorate cookies or make a
avorite dessert? Did you prepare specific items for a holiday meal? What other food items
vere notable this year?

_____

_____

_____

_____

_____

Vhat events and special parties led up to the holiday this year? Did you have any special
elebrations or ceremonies to attend?

_____

_____

_____

FIRST TO WAKE CHRISTMAS MORNING:

FAVORITE GIFT OF THE SEASON:

MISHAP MOMENT:

SPECIAL ORNAMENT THIS YEAR:

Christmas Archive

How did you spend Christmas Eve and Christmas Day? Which family and friends were in attendance?

_____

_____

_____

_____

_____

Talk about your outfits and attire this year. Did you do family jammies? Were there special dresses or suits worn to your celebrations?

_____

_____

_____

_____

_____

Let's talk gifts. Were there any favorites this year or anything given or recieved that helped make this Christmas special?

_____

_____

_____

_____

_____

CHRISTMAS BOOK THIS YEAR:

CHRISTMAS SONG THIS YEAR:

CHRISTMAS MOVIE THIS YEAR:

TOP NEWS HEADLINE THIS YEAR:

Describe your new and old family traditions this year.

Use this space to describe your favorite holiday memory from this season.

Christmas Archive

PASTE YOUR HOLIDAY PHOTOS OR CARD HERE

Made in the USA
Columbia, SC
28 November 2020